Events of the Revolution

George Rogers Clark:
War in the West

By Susan and John Lee

Illustrated by Richard Wahl

 CHILDRENS PRESS, CHICAGO

Library of Congress Cataloging in Publication Da[ta]

Lee, Susan.
  George Rogers Clark: War in the West.
  (Events of the Revolution)
  SUMMARY: Follows the campaigns of Major
Rogers Clark whose small army of Virginians cap[tured]
several frontier forts for the colonists during the
Revolution.
  1. Clark, George Rogers, 1752-1818—Juvenile
literature. 2. Northwest, Old—History—Revolutio[n]
1775-1783—Juvenile literature. [1. Clark, George
Rogers, 1752-1818. 2. United States—History—
Revolution, 1775-1783] I. Lee, John, joint author.
II. Wahl, Richard, 1939-   III. Title.
E207.C5L4   973.3′3′0924 [B]   75-979
ISBN 0-516-04676-4

Chapter 1
KENTUCKY COUNTRY

Four men walked into the log fort at Harrod's Town, Kentucky. They looked hungry and mean. Each carried a long hunting rifle. Each wore buckskin hunting clothes.

The tall redhead and the two ragged men went into a log cabin. The man everyone called the Old Man sat by the door. A boy walked up to the cabin. The Old Man put his leg across the door.

"Left my drum inside," said the boy.

"Get it later," said the Old Man.

"Something big going on in there?" he asked.

"Big or little," said the Old Man, "it's not for you or me to know about. Not yet anyway."

"I'll get my drum later," said the boy.

"You do that," said the Old Man.

The three men inside were Ben Linn, Sam Moore, and George Rogers Clark. "Good to be back in Kentucky," said thin, dark Ben Linn. "Haven't been to church since you sent us to Illinois country."

"There was a church in Kaskaskia," said Moore.

"That was a Catholic church, Sam," said Linn, "and you know I'm not Catholic."

The tall redhead said, "Tell me about those Illinois forts. I already know the French in those river towns are good Catholics."

"Why Major Clark," said Moore, "Ben can talk four Indian languages. He can talk English and some French. He can't read, but he sure can talk. Ben, you tell him about those forts."

"We went down the Salt River," said Linn. "Crossed the Ohio near the Wabash. Saw lots of Indian sign. Didn't want to run into *them*, so we took a canoe. Went down the Ohio to the Mississippi."

"Then we went up the Mississippi to Kaskaskia. Got there May 25th. Saw the head Frenchman. He gave us a job pot-hunting."

"You hunted deermeat for the French?" The big redhead smiled, "Kind of risky, wasn't it?"

"Sure," said Linn, "but we got what you wanted by hunting. We got drawings of the towns and forts."

"What about English soldiers?" asked Clark.

"That's the best part, major," said Moore. "There ain't any. No English soldiers at Kaskaskia or at Cahokia. Not a one."

"The fort at Kaskaskia is in bad shape," said Linn. "There's French militia in both places. They may fight us or they might join us. Those French don't have any good reason to fight anyone. Now, the Indians are a different story. They won't fight us alone. But if the English or French fight us, the Indians will help them."

"What about Vincennes?" asked Clark.

"Don't know," said Moore. "Some French said there was 300 or 400 English up there. Some said there was only a few English. No one knows for sure. One thing we do know . . . there's plenty of Indians everywhere."

The meeting broke up. Ben Linn went to church. Sam Moore went to find some rum. Major Clark went off to think and plan.

Harrod's Town, Kentucky was part of Virginia. Virginia was a state in the United States of America. The Americans were fighting a war of independence against England. Most of the fighting was in the states along the Atlantic coast.

Once France had owned Canada and most of

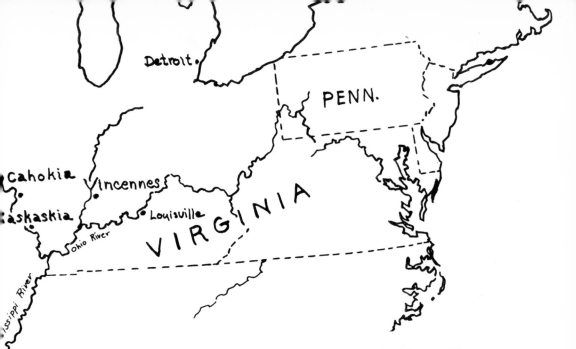

the land along the upper Mississippi River. Part
of that land was called the Illinois country.
Kaskaskia, Cahokia, and Vincennes had been
French trading towns in Illinois country. France
and England had fought what was called the
French and Indian War. France lost and had to
give her land in North America to England.
Kaskaskia, Cahokia, and Vincennes were now
English. The people still spoke French, but they
were ruled by the English.

The main English fort in the west was
Detroit. (In the 1770's, the west stopped at the
Mississippi River.) The English at Detroit gave
guns to the Indians. The Indians raided
Kentucky. They burned farms. They killed and
scalped many American settlers.

The Indians took the scalps to Detroit. The English gave them gunpowder, rum, and presents for the scalps. With the help of the Indians, the English hoped to drive the settlers out of Kentucky.

In the summer of 1777, Major Clark wrote to Patrick Henry, governor of Virginia. He wrote that he had a plan for stopping the Indian war parties. He said he would come and tell the governor about his plan.

On October 1, 1777, Major Clark started for Virginia. He crossed the Cumberland Mountains into Powell's Valley. From there he crossed the Blue Ridge Mountains into Virginia. On November 1, he spent two days at his father's farm. Three days later, he was in Williamsburg, the state captial.

Governor Henry liked Clark's plan to capture the three towns in Illinois country. So did Thomas Jefferson. If those towns were captured, the Indian attacks might stop. The Americans might even be able to capture Detroit. Clark was made a colonel in the Virginia army.

Chapter 2
THE REDHEAD'S ARMY

Clark was now a colonel, but he didn't have an army. The regular Virginia army was with General Washington. Governor Henry told Clark to get his own army.

That was all right with Colonel Clark. He wanted a special army of hunters and Indian fighters. He wanted men who knew how to live in the woods. He wanted men who owned hunting rifles. Men who could hit a deer at 200 yards.

Colonel Clark spent some time in western Virginia. He got some men from the mountain farms. They had fought Indians before. He told them they were going to fight Indians in Kentucky. He didn't tell them of his plans for the Illinois country.

Clark and his men marched up to Fort Pitt. There he got more men. These were tough Pennsylvania hunters and traders. They had been fighting the Indians for years. He didn't tell them about Illinois.

Clark had sent a man back to Kentucky. This man was to get some of the Kentucky settlers to join Clark. The colonel told the man where and when to meet him. He didn't tell this man anything about Illinois. Clark was keeping that part of his plan to himself. He didn't want the English to have any idea where he was going.

Colonel Clark bought gunpowder for his army. He bought lead for bullets. He bought dried corn and bacon. He bought four, big flatboats. Each would carry fifty or more men. The supplies were loaded on the boats. The men climbed in and pushed off.

Each day the flatboats floated further down the Ohio River. The men shot a few deer and ate them for supper. The boats floated along until they got to the Falls of the Ohio (modern Louisville). There Colonel Clark got bad news.

Only about 30 men had come from Kentucky to join him. Clark had hoped for 200. He moved his little army onto Corn Island. It was in the river above the Falls. The army would be safe there. He could train his soldiers on the island without being seen.

He told the men they were going into Illinois country. He told them Illinois was English. He told them he wanted to capture Kaskaskia. Then he let the men talk about his plans. Most of the soldiers liked the idea. Some didn't like it at all.

The Old Man and the boy with the drum had come down from Harrod's Town. The boy was all for going to Kaskaskia. "Why not?" he asked. "We came to fight didn't we?"

"Boy," said the Old Man, "do you know what you're saying? You want to go into Illinois country? There aren't any Americans there. We got no towns there. No forts. No farms to get food from. That country will be alive with Indians. There'll be a thousand French militia. And no one knows how many English soldiers.

You sure you want to stick your head into that bee's nest?"

"Old Man," said the boy, "I've got a drum. I've got my pa's rifle. My pa and ma's scalps are in Detroit. Every army needs a drummer boy. I've got the only drum on this island. I'm going!"

"That rifle's bigger than you are," said the Old Man. "Your drum's almost as big."

"I'm going!" said the boy. "I'm scared, but I'm going."

"All right. Guess I might as well go, too. You just might lose your drumming sticks. If you do, I'll cut you some new ones with old pigsticker here." The Old Man patted his long knife.

Most of the army felt like the Old Man and the boy. They told Colonel Clark they'd be proud to go to Kaskaskia with him. The ones who didn't want to go went down to the river. They swam across and never came back.

The 178-man army loaded into their four flatboats. They ran the white water of the Falls on June 24, 1778. Four days later they picked up some American hunters. The hunters said the French at Kaskaskia hadn't heard of Clark's army. No one there knew that France was helping the Americans in the war.

Clark stopped at old Fort Massacre. The fort hadn't been used for years. The soldiers hid the flatboats near the fort. Kaskaskia was 120 miles away. The men moved out one after the other, Indian style. Each man had his rifle, his food,

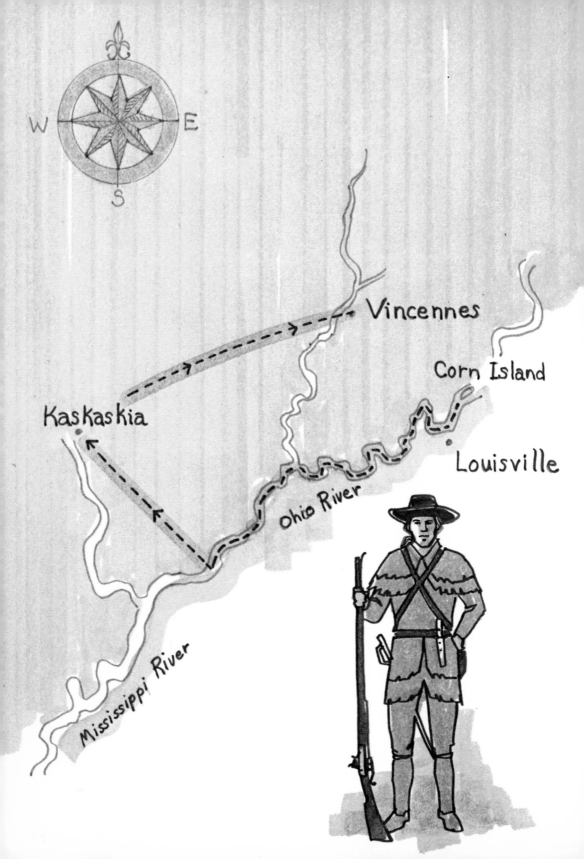

W

E

S

Vincennes

Corn Island

Kaskaskia

Louisville

Ohio River

Mississippi River

and his blanket. For three days they moved through a forest. Then they came to a prairie (tall grass growing on open, rolling flat land).

Their food ran out, so they lived on berries. They got lost once, but found their way again. They met no Indians. Then they came to the Kaskaskia River. Across the river they could see the fort and the town. Along both sides of the river were farms.

When it was dark, Clark's men moved into a French farmyard. The farmer told them the town didn't know they were coming. He told them there were boats down by the river. The Americans found the boats and began to cross the river. Two hours later, Clark and his army were outside Kaskaskia.

Colonel Clark split his men into two groups. He was to lead one group to the fort. The other group was to capture the town.

Clark led his men through the dark to the fort. The gate by the river was open. Was it a trap? The men slipped inside. It wasn't a trap. Clark and a few men slipped into the acting governor's house. He was asleep. Clark woke him and told him the Americans had captured the fort.

The other group went down the streets of the town. They shouted to the French to stay inside their houses. The French stayed inside. Kaskaskia was taken. Not a shot was fired. No one was hurt.

Chapter 3
THE RED BELT OR THE WHITE

"Boy," said the Old Man, "you know what yesterday was?"

"Nope, and I don't care," said the boy, "but I'll bet you're going to tell me anyway."

"Fourth of July it was. Two years since the Declaration of Independence."

The boy beat a roll on his drum. "Hooray for that other Virginia redhead, Thomas Jefferson. You think these French ever heard of him or the Declaration?"

"Clark's got them all in their church over there," said the Old Man. "Maybe he's reading it to them."

Colonel Clark wasn't in the church, but all the French were. They were scared of Clark's "Big Knives." They thought the Big Knives might burn their town. They sent their priest, Father Gibault, to talk to Clark. Six old men went with the priest. They told Clark they wanted to be friends with the Americans.

Clark asked if they knew France was helping America. They didn't. It was true, Clark said. He hadn't come to burn their town. They were still free people. They could do what they wanted. He said the Americans had come as friends.

The priest and the six men went back to the church. The priest told the people what Clark had said. The church bells rang. The people ran into the streets. They shook hands with the Big Knives. "Liberty!" they shouted, "Liberty!"

Later that day Clark sent soldiers to Cahokia. A group of French went with the Big Knives. The next day Cahokia became an American town. Not a shot was fired. No one was hurt.

Now Clark had to worry about Vincennes. It was 200 miles away on the Wabash River. It was the last town between Clark and Detroit. Clark had to capture this town before he could attack Detroit.

Father Gibault had a plan. He said the French had not fought at Kaskaskia or Cahokia. He did not think they would fight at Vincennes. Why not let him go to Vincennes first? He would talk to the people. He thought they would welcome the Americans.

Clark agreed and Father Gibault set out. Two weeks later he was back with good news. The French would welcome the Americans. Even the Indians wanted to smoke a pipe of peace with Clark.

Clark sent Captain Helm and a few men to Vincennes. The French opened the fort for them. Helm knew Indians and their ways. He smoked the peace pipe and talked friendship with the nearby tribes.

More good luck came at the end of the summer. A rider came in from Cahokia. The Indians wanted to meet there with Clark. The colonel set out that night with some of his soldiers. The Old Man and the boy went, too. They got to Cahokia the next day.

"Whooee," said the boy. "Look at all those Indians. I can see teepees for miles. I never saw so many horses or dogs."

"There's many an Indian tribe here," said the Old Man. "Those tall ones are Chippewa.

They come from up past Detroit. There's Kickapoos from out west of the Mississippi. There's Miamis from over in Ohio. There must be 20, maybe 30, Indian tribes here. Colonel Clark will have to put on some kind of show to keep them from lifting our scalps."

The next day the chiefs of the tribes came to see Colonel Clark. They carried red belts of wampum (little beads sewed into a belt). These were belts of war given them by the English. The chiefs made speeches. They said bad birds (the English) gave them the belts. They said they wanted peace with the Big Knives. They threw the red belts on the ground. They stomped on the belts.

Colonel Clark made a short speech. He said he would think about peace. He would come back to the chiefs' fire in two days. They would know his thoughts at that time. That night and the next day, Clark stayed in his cabin.

The Indians talked among themselves. What will the Big Redhair do? Will he want war or peace? Then they heard music. The Big Redhair was leading his people in a dance.

"Clark's a smart one," said the Old Man. "He's dancing in there like he's in a Virginia town. The Indians will think that is a good sign. He's setting them up for his speech tomorrow."

"I don't get it," said the boy. "If he wants peace, why doesn't he just say so?"

"Cause he's smarter than you about Indians. He kept them thinking for a day. Now he's giving them a sign. The Indians will think he wants peace. Tomorrow he will tell them he wants peace. Then the Indians will say they knew it all the time. They will say they read the signs right."

"What will happen then?"

"Then Clark will tell *them* to choose war or peace. He'll say he will be happy to fight or be friends. He'll make them say *they* want to be friends. That's what our cool colonel will do."

The next day Clark stood in front of the chiefs' fire. He held up his right hand. He

shook a red belt of wampum. "In this hand I carry war," he said. He held up his left hand. He shook a white belt in it. "In this hand I carry peace."

Then Clark made a speech. He talked of the English and the Americans. He talked of how the English hired Indians to fight for them. He talked of how the French were helping the Americans. He talked of how the Americans would beat the English. He talked of how the Americans would not ask the Indians to fight for them. He said the Americans could do their own fighting.

Then he said, "Here is a bloody belt and a white one. Take the one you want." That night the Indians talked among themselves. The next day the Indians took the white belt. The pipe of peace was smoked. The Indians and Big Knives were at peace.

Chapter 4
THE WATER ROAD

A French runner trotted into the fort at Detroit. Colonel Henry Hamilton of the English army was about to get some bad news.

"Kaskaskia, Cahokia, Vincennes," the runner said, "the Americans have captured all three."

Hamilton knew he had to get these towns back. He got his army ready. He loaded 175 soldiers and 350 Indians into boats. They went down the Detroit River into Lake Erie. They cut across the west end of the lake. They poled up the Maumee River. By late October they were at the nine-mile portage (a land crossing between two rivers).

For a day they carried their boats and supplies the nine miles to the Wabash River. Then they went down that river toward Vincennes. Over 200 Indians joined them on the way. The week before Christmas, 1778, Hamilton's army captured Vincennes. Captain Helm and his few men were prisoners.

Hamilton learned that Clark had 80 men in Kaskaskia and 40 in Cahokia. He knew the rivers between his army and Clark's were flooded. He didn't think he could move his army 200 miles in the winter. So Hamilton settled down to spend the winter in Vincennes. Most of the Indians went back to their homes. They could wipe out the Americans in the spring.

Now it was Clark's turn to get bad news. A trader told him that Hamilton had captured Vincennes. For some time, Clark didn't do anything.

The boy watched the Old Man sharpen his knife. "I don't see what you want that so sharp for," he said. "You won't get to use it this winter."

The Old Man spat in the fire. "Sometimes I think you never learn anything. How long you been with Clark now? You think he'll do what anyone else would do? He'll end up taking us to Vincennes."

"In this snow and ice?" said the boy. "He going to grow duck feathers and fly us up there?"

"You may wish you had feathers before we get there. Now clean your rifle. You're going to need it soon."

Clark and 130 men marched out on February 5, 1779. The boy was beating his drum. But no one tried to stay in step. Ahead lay 200 miles of snow, ice, and flooded prairie. They made six miles the first day. They ate a cold supper and drank hot tea. They rolled up in their blankets. It rained all night.

The army was on its way before dawn. They marched 27 miles that day. They slept in the rain again. The third day they began wading across the prairie. They shot deer or buffalo

each day for food. They ate well but always they slept in the rain.

"You all right?" asked the Old Man.

"I'll make it," said the boy. "If a skinny Old Man like you can make it, I'll make it."

"If you make it, I'll stop calling you boy. 'Cause if you can make it, you won't be a boy no more."

Each day Clark led the way, as wet and cold as any of his soldiers. A week after they left Kaskaskia, they came to the Little Wabash River. They still had 63 cold, wet, hard miles to go. The river had flooded. It was five miles across to the hills on the far side. Clark checked his men. One out of three was sick from the cold.

Clark had the strongest men cut down poplar trees. From these the men made dugout canoes. The sick men climbed into the canoes. Clark lifted his rifle high and stepped into the river. The men followed him. The water was up to their knees. Then it was up to their belts. Clark

began to sing. Everyone sang. The water grew deeper. The short men had to hang onto the canoes.

"Look at the drummer boy," someone shouted. "That lazy pup is riding his drum." And so he was. The boy was sitting on his drum. He held onto a canoe and it pulled him along.

"He's not a lazy pup," shouted a soldier, "he's a wise old dog."

All made it across the river. They climbed the hill and sat under the trees. They built fires and tried to dry out. They should have been beaten men but they weren't. "We did it," they said. "We beat that flooded river. Anyplace Colonel Clark can lead, we can follow."

The next day they marched through a flooded swamp. Thin ice covered the water. The men waded through the broken ice. That night each man got a handful of dried corn and a cup of tea. On and on they went. Then they reached the Embarrass River. They were close now. They waded along that river until they came to the Wabash River. Vincennes was just nine miles away.

"Camp Hunger, I call it," said the Old Man. "No corn, no meat, no nothing. We'll have to beat the English and eat their food."

"Nine more miles of water," said the boy.

"Nothing to it," said the Old Man. "I'm half fish now. I'm growing scales on my feet."

Clark sent out scouts. The rest of the men made more dugout canoes. At noon the scouts came in with five captured Frenchmen. The Frenchmen said no one knew they were coming. One of the Frenchmen had killed a deer. That night 130 men made supper of that one deer.

The next day the army went back into the water. They waded up to their belts in ice-cold water. All were tired. All were hungry. But no one was going to stop now.

That night they found a little hill to sleep on. At dawn they went back into the water. They were cold and wet. They were tired and hungry. But they were moving. The scouts captured some Indians in a canoe. There was buffalo meat and corn in the canoe. It wasn't a big meal, but everyone got something to chew.

Again they went on. . .on. . .on. . .until they could see Vincennes just two miles ahead.

Chapter 5
ONE FOR EACH STATE

The ducks flew low over the Old Man's head. They circled and came down on the water. BOOM! went a gun. Up went the ducks again.

"Duck hunters!" said the Old Man. "They're in that brush up by the river."

"We need a prisoner," said Colonel Clark. "Take two men and get me one of those duck hunters."

The Old Man pointed at a man and the boy.

Clark looked at the boy and then at the Old Man.

"He's a man now, colonel," said the Old Man. "He made the same trip we made. He's got his rifle and his powder's dry."

"Take him if you want him," said Clark. "Just don't wake up the fort getting the prisoner."

The Old Man led out. "Keep low in the brush," he said. "When we spot a hunter, the boy will stand up and wave. While the hunter is waving back, we'll take him from behind. Now, no more talking."

They moved through the brush like Indians. They spotted a hunter. The Old Man pointed to the left. The boy slipped off to the left. The two men moved up behind the hunter. They lay a few feet from him and waited.

The boy stepped from behind a tree and waved. The hunter stood up and looked at him. Then a hand was over the hunter's mouth. A

sharp knife was under his chin. "Let's go," said the Old Man. "We've got the colonel's prisoner."

Clark talked to the duck hunter. Yes, the man said, Hamilton was at the fort. No, he didn't know the Americans were coming. Yes, there were 200 Indians camped nearby. No, the French wouldn't help the English. They would stay out of the fight.

Clark took out paper, pen, and ink. He wrote a note to the French in the town. He said an American army was going to attack the fort. He told the French to stay in their houses. He said the Americans were friends of the French. Clark gave the note to the hunter and sent him back to town.

Clark had been careful not to let the hunter see how few men he had. Now he had his men cut down 20 thin trees. He tied a red and green flag on each one. Clark could see the French in town looking out at the woods. He had his men march around. The flags could be seen but the men were hidden in the brush.

"Smart," said the Old Man. "We got us a smart colonel. Counting those flags, the French will think he's got a big army out here."

Darkness came. Lights were lit in the houses in Vincennes. Clark moved his men close to town. One group moved up to the fort. One group moved into the town. The French could see men moving in the darkness. A few Indians were in the streets. They said to each other, "The Big Knives have walked on water to get here. Let us watch. We will see who wins, the American Redhair or the English Hairbuyer. Let the white men kill each other."

The Americans moved out of town to join the group by the fort. They hid behind trees. They sat behind fences. They aimed at the fort. The boy beat out a roll on his drum. "Fire!" shouted Clark.

A hundred dots of flame could be seen. A hundred bullets hit the fort. Inside the fort men jumped from bed. Someone blew a bugle. Someone beat a drum. Soon a cannon was fired. The cannonball went through the tops of the trees. The Americans fired at the flame of the cannon. English gunners fell dead in the darkness.

A group of French came from the town. They had hidden their gunpowder from the English. Now they gave it to the Americans. They also brought fresh loaves of bread. Both were needed and Clark thanked the French.

Clark told his men to laugh and shout. He told them to shoot and move. He wanted the English to think he had a big army. Dawn came and Clark told the men to stay hidden. Then he sent a note to the fort. The note ordered the English to surrender.

Colonel Hamilton sent back a note saying he was not about to surrender.

Clark's men began to fire again. They easily picked off the English Redcoats. At noon the sun came out. So did an English soldier. Hamilton wanted to stop the fighting for three days. Clark sent back a note saying "no".

Then an Indian war party came out of the woods. They walked toward the fort. Some were waving scalps and shouting. The Americans captured them. Four of the Indians had scalps of Kentucky men and women. Clark made these four sit by a fence near the fort. The Indians sang their death song. Then the Americans killed them.

The French watched all this. They said nothing. The Indians who were camped nearby watched. They did nothing. The Indians knew killing was part of war. They talked against the English. The English had hired the scalp hunters. The English should have come out of the fort. They should have helped the men they hired.

The sun was going down when the fort gate opened. Colonel Hamilton came out. He and Clark talked. Hamilton knew the French wouldn't help him. He knew the Indians wouldn't help the English now. He told Clark he would surrender the next morning.

The English did march out and surrender. Captain Helm and his men were freed. Americans took over the fort. They fired the cannon 13 times — once for each American state.

"Well, boy," said the Old Man, "we did it. We captured all this land for the United States."

"Don't call me boy. Call me Illinois Jack. I'm a Big Knife, not a drummer boy."

EPILOGUE:

Later, the land Clark and his small army captured became the states of Illinois and Indiana. The English also lost what became Ohio, Michigan, and Wisconsin because of what Clark won.

IMPORTANT DATES OF THE REVOLUTION

1775	April 19	Fighting at Lexington and Concord
	May 10	Ethan Allen captures Fort Ticonderoga
	June 15	George Washington elected commander-in-chief of army
	June 16/17	Battle of Bunker (Breed's) Hill;
	September	American soldiers invade Canada; Ethan Allen captured
	November/ December	British and Americans fight in Canada, South Carolina, New York, Virginia, Maine, and at sea
1776	March 17	British withdraw from Boston
	July 4	Congress adopts the Declaration of Independence
	August 27	Battle of Long Island; Americans retreat
	September 15	British take New York City
	September 16	Americans win Battle of Harlem Heights
	October 11/13	British fleet wins Battle of Lake Champlain
	October 28	British win at White Plains, N. Y.
	November 16	British take Fort Washington
	November 28	British take Rhode Island
	December	Washington takes army across Delaware and into Pennsylvania
	December 26	Washington wins Battle of Trenton, New Jersey
1777	January 3	Americans win Battle of Princeton
	January	American army winters at Morristown, New Jersey
	August 6	Battle of Oriskany, N. Y.
	August 16	Americans win Battle of Bennington, Vt.
	September 11	British win Battle of Brandywine
	September 26	British occupy Philadelphia
	October 4	British win Battle of Germantown
	October 6	British capture Forts Clinton and Montgomery
	October 7	Battles of Saratoga, N. Y.; British General Burgoyne's army surrenders October 17
	November 15	Articles of Confederation adopted
	December 18	Washington's army winters at Valley Forge

'78	February 6	France signs treaty of alliance with America
	June 18	British evacuate Philadelphia
	June 28	Americans win Battle of Monmouth Court House, N.J.
	July 4	George Rogers Clark wins at Kaskaskia
	August 29	Battle of Rhode Island; Americans retreat
	December 29	British capture Savannah, Ga.
'79	January	British take Vincennes, Ind.
	February 3	British lose at Charles Town, S. C.
	February 14	Americans win at Kettle Creek, Ga.
	February 20	Americans capture Vincennes
	March 3	British win at Briar Creek, Ga.
	June 20	Americans lose at Stono Ferry, S.C.
	July 16	Americans take Fort Stony Point, N. Y.
	August/ September	Fighting continues on land and sea. On September 23 John Paul Jones captures British *Serapis*
	December	Americans winter at Morristown, N.J.
'80	May 12	Charles Town surrenders to British
	June 20	Battle of Ramsour's Mills, N. C.
	July 30	Battle of Rocky Mount, S. C.
	September 26	Battle of Charlotte, N. C.
	October 7	Battle of King's Mountain, S. C.
'81	January 17	Americans win Battle of Cowpens, S. C.
	March/April	Battles in North Carolina, South Carolina, Virginia, Georgia
	October 19	British army surrenders at Yorktown
'82	July 11	British leave Savannah, Ga.
	November 30	Preliminary peace signed between America and Britain
	December 14	British leave Charleston, S. C.
'83	September 3	Final peace treaty signed
	November 25	British evacuate New York City

About the Authors:

Susan Dye Lee has been writing professionally since she graduated from college in 1961. Working with the Social Studies Curriculum Center at Northwestern University, she has created course materials in American studies. Ms. Lee has also co-authored a text on Latin America and Canada, written case studies in legal history for the Law in American Society Project, and developed a teacher's guide for tapes that explore women's role in America's past. The writer credits her students for many of her ideas. Currently, she is doing research for her history dissertation on the Women's Christian Temperance Union for Northwestern University. In her free moments, Susan Lee enjoys traveling, playing the piano, and welcoming friends to "Highland Cove," the summer cottage she and her husband, John, share.

John R. Lee enjoys a prolific career as a writer, teacher, and outdoorsman. After receiving his doctorate in social studies at Stanford, Dr. Lee came to Northwestern University's School of Education, where he advises student teachers and directs graduates in training. A versatile writer, Dr. Lee has co-authored the Scott-Foresman social studies textbooks for primary-age children. In addition, he has worked on the production of 50 films and over 100 filmstrips. His biographical film on Helen Keller received a 1970 Venice Film Festival award. His college text, *Teaching Social Studies in the Elementary School*, has recently been published. Besides pro-football, Dr. Lee's passion is his Wisconsin cottage, where he likes to shingle leaky roofs, split wood, and go sailing.

About the Artist

Richard Wahl, graduate of the Art Center College of Design in Los Angeles, has illustrated a number of magazine articles and booklets. He is a skilled artist and photographer who advocates realistic interpretations of his subjects. He lives with his wife and two sons in Libertyville, Illinois.